About the Creators of This Calendar

Dawn Huffaker is an established poet who has written for more than 35 years. She primarily writes about the incredible beauty in nature. Her goal is to paint a memorable picture with her words. This is her ninth calendar. So far, she has published four books of poetry available at Amazon. Learn more about her at www.dawnhuffaker.com

Dawn is unable to walk. She lives her life from a motorized wheelchair. Doing photography is quite difficult for her. She focuses on her poetry, instead.

Since she is unable to take her own photos, Dawn has been blessed with a family that is very talented with a camera. This year, the calendar includes beautiful nature photography from her parents, Marilyn & Ron Huffaker. They each add much to Dawn's poetry.

The creators hope that you will find even more beauty and magic in this current edition. Enjoy!

New Year

Fireworks flashed
So fast and furious
In rippling frissons
Which flare and flourish.

Cacophonies competed
For concentration and consideration
In clashing waves
That crash and cling.

Craziness celebrated
With claps and kisses
In mounting cheers
That captivate and charm.

Revelers retreated
For rest and repose
In weary reluctance
To reminisce and recall.

Sunrise slid
So softly and silently
In gentle streams
That stir and stimulate.

New Year has begun!

- Dawn L. Huffaker

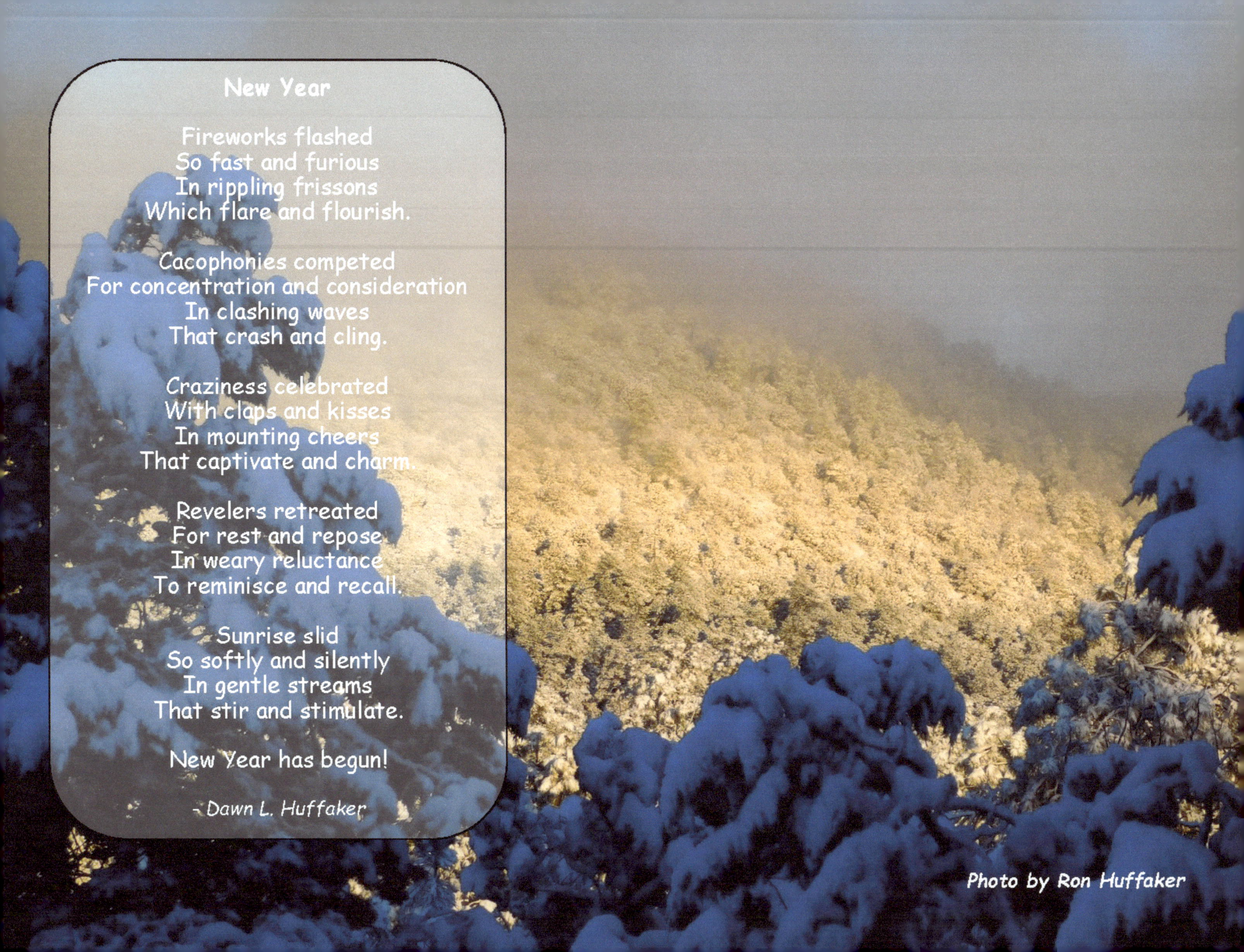

Photo by Ron Huffaker

January 2018

December 2017

S	M	T	W	T	F	S
					1	2
3	4	5	6	7	8	9
10	11	12	13	14	15	16
17	18	19	20	21	22	23
24	25	26	27	28	29	30
31						

February 2018

S	M	T	W	T	F	S
				1	2	3
4	5	6	7	8	9	10
11	12	13	14	15	16	17
18	19	20	21	22	23	24
25	26	27	28			

Sunday	Monday	Tuesday	Wednesday	Thursday	Friday	Saturday
	1 New Year's Day	2	3	4	5	6
7	8	9	10	11	12	13
14	15 Martin Luther King, Jr., Day	16	17	18	19	20
21	22	23	24	25	26	27
28	29	30	31			

Soft Air

Winter releases its icy hold on
World below.
Warm spring sings songs while
Waking flora to rise to sky.

Soft air brushes by
Satin petals newly born.
Sweet fragrance wafts when
Supple branches sway.

Lively bees glide on
Lithe wings newly born.
Loving sighs speak volumes when
Luscious pollen to legs attach.

Cycles within cycles
Changing seasons flow.
Complete mastery shines when
Cherished spring sleeps no more.

Dawn L. Huffaker

Photo by Ron Huffaker

February 2018

January 2018						
S	M	T	W	T	F	S
	1	2	3	4	5	6
7	8	9	10	11	12	13
14	15	16	17	18	19	20
21	22	23	24	25	26	27
28	29	30	31			

March 2018						
S	M	T	W	T	F	S
				1	2	3
4	5	6	7	8	9	10
11	12	13	14	15	16	17
18	19	20	21	22	23	24
25	26	27	28	29	30	31

Sunday	Monday	Tuesday	Wednesday	Thursday	Friday	Saturday
				1 National Freedom Day	2 Groundhog Day	3
4	5	6	7	8	9	10
11	12 Lincoln's Birthday	13 Mardi Gras	14 Ash Wednesday Valentine's Day	15 Susan B. Anthony Day	16	17
18	19 President's Day	20	21	22 Washington's Birthday	23	24
25	26	27	28			

Snow Fell

Snow fell in the silence of the night.
Winter was not so ready to leave.
He encased the young, tender branches
In immobilizing, icy, white sheaths.

Where is the promise of spring?
Where did the warmth of the sun go?
How many blossoms were damaged?
How long will it stay cold?

The snow is not very deep.
Temperature is barely cold enough.
Snow will not stay long.
Spring is only hiding in the shadows.

Soon she will regroup and reign again.
This will be a distant memory
To be shared among the flowers
On a hot, steamy day in July.

- Dawn L. Huffaker

March 2018

Sunday	Monday	Tuesday	Wednesday	Thursday	Friday	Saturday
				1	2	3
4	5	6	7	8	9	10
11 Daylight Saving Begins	12	13	14	15	16	17 St. Patrick's Day
18	19	20	21 Spring Begins	22	23	24
25 Palm Sunday	26	27	28	29	30 Good Friday	31

Painted Tulips

Painted tulips with
Swirls of snowy white
And candy-cane pink
Gently bob to the breeze.

They peer up to the sky
In hopes of seeing the sun.
Sunlight falls in dappled patterns
Through the new tree leaves above.

This changing light
Makes the petals glow like
Chinese lanterns slowly drifting
Down a stream during a festival.

What magic there is in spring!
New life is starting everywhere!
Painted tulips are curious and eager
To experience it all!

- Dawn L. Huffaker

April 2018

Sunday	Monday	Tuesday	Wednesday	Thursday	Friday	Saturday
1 **Easter Sunday** **April Fool's Day**	2	3	4	5	6	7
8	9	10	11	12	13	14
15	16	17	18	19	20	21
22 **Earth Day**	23	24	25 **Administrative Assistant's Day**	26	27 **Arbor Day**	28
29	30					

Night Wandering

Young bear follows the deer trail
Seeing where it will take him.
Tantalizing smells are all about.
He's checked out the nearest trash cans.
They were sealed tight. Bummer!
His belly is still grumbling at him,

Other smells, off in the distance,
Call him to come check them out.
He wanders on down the trail
Further into the sleeping mountain town.
Perhaps, he can scarf down
Some tasty dog food by a door.

Onward, ever onward,
Young bear saunters on.

- Dawn L. Huffaker

Photo by Ron Huffaker

May 2018

April 2018

S	M	T	W	T	F	S
1	2	3	4	5	6	7
8	9	10	11	12	13	14
15	16	17	18	19	20	21
22	23	24	25	26	27	28
29	30					

June 2018

S	M	T	W	T	F	S
					1	2
3	4	5	6	7	8	9
10	11	12	13	14	15	16
17	18	19	20	21	22	23
24	25	26	27	28	29	30

Sunday	Monday	Tuesday	Wednesday	Thursday	Friday	Saturday
		1	2	3	4	5 Cinco de Mayo
6	7	8 National Teacher Day	9	10	11	12
13 Mother's Day	14	15	16	17	18	19 Armed Forces Day
20	21	22 National Maritime Day	23	24	25	26
27	28 Memorial Day	29	30	31		

Cosmos Revel

Hot summer sun shines down
From high above.
Cosmos revel in this heat.
Growing taller by the day.
Seeking to touch the sky.

Baby buds swell and swell.
Hoping they will open soon.
Wind jostles them to and fro to help.
Finally, they burst forth like
Popcorn on a stove flame.

Hummingbirds hover around
The new blossom additions of
Crimson red, neon pink and cool white -
Savoring each sweet nectar they taste.
Looking forward to much more.

- Dawn L. Huffaker

Photo by Marilyn Huffaker

June 2018

<table>
<tr><td colspan="7">

May 2018

S	M	T	W	T	F	S
		1	2	3	4	5
6	7	8	9	10	11	12
13	14	15	16	17	18	19
20	21	22	23	24	25	26
27	28	29	30	31		

</td></tr>
</table>

July 2018

S	M	T	W	T	F	S
1	2	3	4	5	6	7
8	9	10	11	12	13	14
15	16	17	18	19	20	21
22	23	24	25	26	27	28
29	30	31				

Sunday	Monday	Tuesday	Wednesday	Thursday	Friday	Saturday
					1	2
3	4	5	6	7	8	9
10	11	12	13	14 Flag Day	15	16
17 Father's Day	18	19	20	21 Summer Begins	22	23
24	25	26	27	28	29	30

Mycelia Awaken

Monsoon raindrops
Fall from on high.
Icy cold, they are,
When ground they touch.

Soak, they do,
Dirt so dry and almost lifeless.
Mycelia eagerly awaken underground.
Mysteriously, fruits break through.

Colorful mushrooms rise slowly
From this monsoon-moistened soil.
Opening like ancient parasols,
They spread spores, their future, to the air.

Nature's way to propagate.

- Dawn L. Huffaker

Photo by Marilyn Huffaker

July 2018

June 2018						
S	M	T	W	T	F	S
					1	2
3	4	5	6	7	8	9
10	11	12	13	14	15	16
17	18	19	20	21	22	23
24	25	26	27	28	29	30

August 2018						
S	M	T	W	T	F	S
			1	2	3	4
5	6	7	8	9	10	11
12	13	14	15	16	17	18
19	20	21	22	23	24	25
26	27	28	29	30	31	

Sunday	Monday	Tuesday	Wednesday	Thursday	Friday	Saturday
1	2	3	4 Independence Day	5	6	7
8	9	10	11	12	13	14
15	16	17	18	19	20	21
22 Parent's Day	23	24	25	26	27	28
29	30	31				

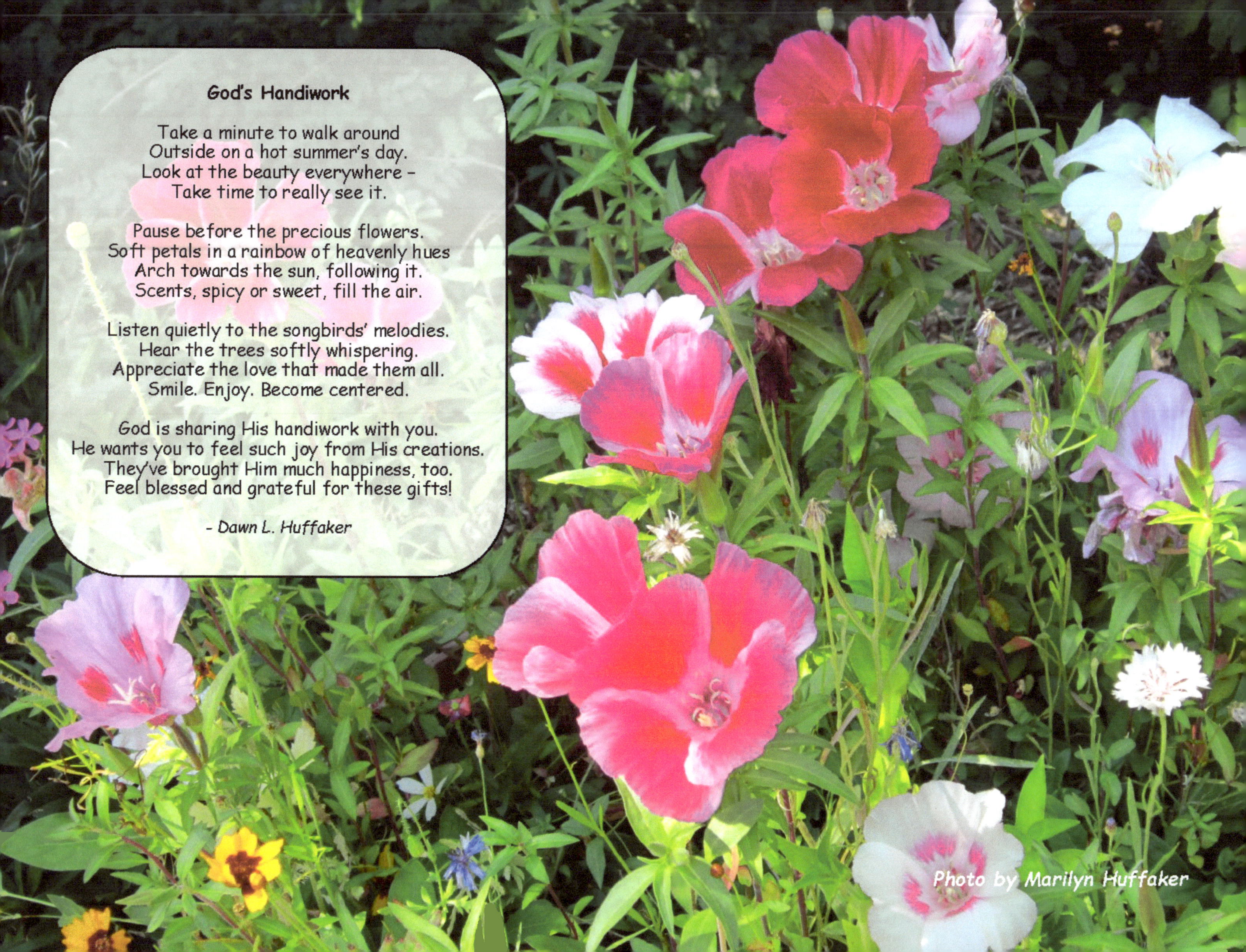

God's Handiwork

Take a minute to walk around
Outside on a hot summer's day.
Look at the beauty everywhere –
Take time to really see it.

Pause before the precious flowers.
Soft petals in a rainbow of heavenly hues
Arch towards the sun, following it.
Scents, spicy or sweet, fill the air.

Listen quietly to the songbirds' melodies.
Hear the trees softly whispering.
Appreciate the love that made them all.
Smile. Enjoy. Become centered.

God is sharing His handiwork with you.
He wants you to feel such joy from His creations.
They've brought Him much happiness, too.
Feel blessed and grateful for these gifts!

- Dawn L. Huffaker

August 2018

July 2018						
S	M	T	W	T	F	S
1	2	3	4	5	6	7
8	9	10	11	12	13	14
15	16	17	18	19	20	21
22	23	24	25	26	27	28
29	30	31				

September 2018						
S	M	T	W	T	F	S
						1
2	3	4	5	6	7	8
9	10	11	12	13	14	15
16	17	18	19	20	21	22
23	24	25	26	27	28	29
30						

Sunday	Monday	Tuesday	Wednesday	Thursday	Friday	Saturday
			1	2	3	4
5	6	7	8	9	10	11
12	13	14	15	16	17	18
19	20	21	22	23	24	25
26	27	28	29	30	31	

Evening Draws Near

Fawn is hungry again.
Pausing from her grazing,
She lets him nurse.
He is growing quickly.
One day this will be a memory.

For now, the world becomes still.
It is just the two of them.
She nuzzles him tenderly.
Her ears still swivel to listen for trouble.
Her eyes carefully watch for predators.

Their peaceful moment might end.
It could shatter in an instant.
Legs tense to push off to flee.
Head off in the opposite direction.
Leaving trouble behind is their goal.

Until then, all is right with the world,
As evening draws near.

- Dawn L. Huffaker

Photo by Ron Huffaker

September 2018

August 2018

S	M	T	W	T	F	S
			1	2	3	4
5	6	7	8	9	10	11
12	13	14	15	16	17	18
19	20	21	22	23	24	25
26	27	28	29	30	31	

October 2018

S	M	T	W	T	F	S
	1	2	3	4	5	6
7	8	9	10	11	12	13
14	15	16	17	18	19	20
21	22	23	24	25	26	27
28	29	30	31			

Sunday	Monday	Tuesday	Wednesday	Thursday	Friday	Saturday
						1
2	3 Labor Day	4	5	6	7	8
9 Grandparent's Day	10	11	12	13	14	15
16	17 Citizenship Day	18	19	20	21	22 Autumn Begins
23	24	25	26	27	28	29
30						

Luna

Day is done.
Work has ceased.
Sun slumbers beyond.
Luna lifts her head.
It is the time to rise.

The stars carry her above.
Moonlight shimmers delicately
Among the tree branches and leaves.
Forest floor has patterns appearing in this
Ocean of light and jet-black shadows.

Moonrise is ancient.
It is ever thus.
And yet, it mesmerizes the onlooker.
It calls to a simpler time
When wonder and magic reigned.

- Dawn L. Huffaker

Photo by Ron Huffaker

October 2018

September 2018

S	M	T	W	T	F	S
						1
2	3	4	5	6	7	8
9	10	11	12	13	14	15
16	17	18	19	20	21	22
23	24	25	26	27	28	29
30						

November 2018

S	M	T	W	T	F	S
				1	2	3
4	5	6	7	8	9	10
11	12	13	14	15	16	17
18	19	20	21	22	23	24
25	26	27	28	29	30	

Sunday	Monday	Tuesday	Wednesday	Thursday	Friday	Saturday
	1	2	3	4	5	6
7	8 **Columbus Day**	9	10	11	12	13
14	15	16	17	18	19	20
21	22	23	24 **United Nations Day**	25	26	27
28	29	30	31 **Halloween**			

Celebration

Must hurry!
Getting dressed in our finery.
Mustn't forget the headdresses!
Don't we look so wonderful?

I can hear the flute and drum!
The others are heading out.
Checking one last time
To see that everything is in order.

With a nod to the children,
We leave to catch up to the others.
Everyone looks so nice.
This is going to be a grand party!

Bobbing quail heads lead the way.
A Thanksgiving feast is about to take place.
All have brought seeds and nuts,
Grateful for the harvest of the summer past.

- Dawn L. Huffaker

November 2018

October 2018
S M T W T F S
1 2 3 4 5 6
7 8 9 10 11 12 13
14 15 16 17 18 19 20
21 22 23 24 25 26 27
28 29 30 31

December 2018
S M T W T F S
1
2 3 4 5 6 7 8
9 10 11 12 13 14 15
16 17 18 19 20 21 22
23 24 25 26 27 28 29
30 31

Sunday	Monday	Tuesday	Wednesday	Thursday	Friday	Saturday
				1	2	3
4 **Daylight Saving Ends**	5	6	7	8	9	10
11	12 **Veterans Day**	13	14	15	16	17
18	19	20	21	22 **Thanksgiving Day**	23	24
25	26	27	28	29	30	

Morning Bright

A crisp, cold, calm
Has come with the morn.
Snowy puffs have settled all around.
Nothing moves.

Although it is peaceful and still,
There is an energy of love
Which calls to the hearts of
Mortal man.

For this is the day
To celebrate the birth
Of our Lord and Savior,
Who loves us so very much!

With the mind's eye,
Can you see the Star in the East?
Can you see the Babe in the manger?
No time can separate us. No distance either.

Merry Christmas & Happy New Year!

- Dawn L. Huffaker

December 2018

Sunday	Monday	Tuesday	Wednesday	Thursday	Friday	Saturday
						1
2	3	4	5	6	7	8
9	10	11	12	13	14	15 **Bill of Rights Day**
16	17	18	19	20	21 **Winter Begins**	22
23	24 **Christmas Eve**	25 **Christmas Day**	26	27	28	29
30	31 **New Year's Eve**					

2018

January 2018

S	M	T	W	T	F	S
	1	2	3	4	5	6
7	8	9	10	11	12	13
14	15	16	17	18	19	20
21	22	23	24	25	26	27
28	29	30	31			

February 2018

S	M	T	W	T	F	S
				1	2	3
4	5	6	7	8	9	10
11	12	13	14	15	16	17
18	19	20	21	22	23	24
25	26	27	28			

March 2018

S	M	T	W	T	F	S
				1	2	3
4	5	6	7	8	9	10
11	12	13	14	15	16	17
18	19	20	21	22	23	24
25	26	27	28	29	30	31

April 2018

S	M	T	W	T	F	S
1	2	3	4	5	6	7
8	9	10	11	12	13	14
15	16	17	18	19	20	21
22	23	24	25	26	27	28
29	30					

May 2018

S	M	T	W	T	F	S
		1	2	3	4	5
6	7	8	9	10	11	12
13	14	15	16	17	18	19
20	21	22	23	24	25	26
27	28	29	30	31		

June 2018

S	M	T	W	T	F	S
					1	2
3	4	5	6	7	8	9
10	11	12	13	14	15	16
17	18	19	20	21	22	23
24	25	26	27	28	29	30

July 2018

S	M	T	W	T	F	S
1	2	3	4	5	6	7
8	9	10	11	12	13	14
15	16	17	18	19	20	21
22	23	24	25	26	27	28
29	30	31				

August 2018

S	M	T	W	T	F	S
			1	2	3	4
5	6	7	8	9	10	11
12	13	14	15	16	17	18
19	20	21	22	23	24	25
26	27	28	29	30	31	

September 2018

S	M	T	W	T	F	S
						1
2	3	4	5	6	7	8
9	10	11	12	13	14	15
16	17	18	19	20	21	22
23	24	25	26	27	28	29
30						

October 2018

S	M	T	W	T	F	S
	1	2	3	4	5	6
7	8	9	10	11	12	13
14	15	16	17	18	19	20
21	22	23	24	25	26	27
28	29	30	31			

November 2018

S	M	T	W	T	F	S
				1	2	3
4	5	6	7	8	9	10
11	12	13	14	15	16	17
18	19	20	21	22	23	24
25	26	27	28	29	30	

December 2018

S	M	T	W	T	F	S
						1
2	3	4	5	6	7	8
9	10	11	12	13	14	15
16	17	18	19	20	21	22
23	24	25	26	27	28	29
30	31					